Beyond the Bottle:

9 Powerful Strategies to Reclaim Your Life!

CLAY CUTTS

a.k.a. Sergeant Sober

ISBN-13: 978-1511634519
ISBN-10: 1511634510

DEDICATION

This book is dedicated to my wife, Carolyn, who has patiently put up with a million crazy ideas, a thousand half-finished projects and countless late nights working on "who-knows-what". Thank you, My Love!

CONTENTS

ACKNOWLEDGMENTS

I would like to thank the millions of men and women who came before me and did the thing of which they were most afraid. Without their courage I could never have found my voice. I want to offer a special thanks to Steve Brossman and Tom Beal…ya'll know why!

FOREWORD

<u>Change Your Family Tree</u>

July 12th, 2013 was the day that I took my last drink of alcohol. Prior to that, May 4th, 2013 was the last day that I had anything to drink…beers with the guys while playing golf. I remember that May afternoon clearly. We were golfing, playing cards and having one more beer, then another. I said to myself "I am 40 years old and tired…I don't *want* another beer!" It all washed over me in an instant, like an unexpected wave that catches a kid running off guard. The wave crashed, I stood up and collected myself, and was convinced that I just did not want to drink any more. So what happened in July? My wife and I shared a bottle of wine while celebrating our 17th wedding anniversary. The next morning I felt like a failure because I had let *myself* down. I had not done anything dumb that night…no arguments, no hangover. But the pain I felt was worse because I had failed myself. Why was drinking such a big deal?

My story is a little different than most. I'm not an alcoholic, but based on my family history, I very well could be. My father died in 2006 at 62 from cirrhosis of the liver. He was in fact, an alcoholic in a family tree that had many alcoholic branches, and had been drinking for as long as I could remember. His was not the come home drunk, knock the door in, and slap everybody around kind of drinking; but rather the drink with the guys, have a drink to escape work, occasionally embarrassing at parties, occasional arguments with the wife kind of drinking. In my eyes he was the normal father doing what every man did. Initially, I was sad that he was gone…but then I became angry that he was missing seeing my kids grow up!

I did not let that stop me from continuing my lifestyle of social drinking. Then I was struck by something I read in a book in early 2013, *Every Man's Marriage,* which was given to me by a friend. One piece of the book talks about the importance of *your* impact on your family tree … that the decisions you make today will affect every generation to come, whether it be 5 or 100 years down the road. The writer offers this: "*At some point, every man must decide: Will I purify my branch of the tree, or will I allow this poison to seep through the generations, leaving the job for a better man down the line?*" As I said earlier, that powerful wave finally hit once me. This is is what I finally realized: Most of the dumb decisions I have ever made involved alcohol, 90% of all arguments with my wife were a result of drinking, 99.99% of all **stupid** situations I ever found myself in were a result of alcohol, and if I did not do something to stop the cycle TODAY, then I was not just risking *my* life. I was putting my kids, their kids, and their kids' kids at risk. I could not fathom seeing my children battle alcoholism one day and know that I had steered them there. I had to be the one to purify my branch ... so I did, and I have.

I met Clay Cutts in the late 90s while we were working together at a software company in Greenville, SC. I remember thinking that he was one of the smartest people I had ever met ... he could solve any problem thrown at him ... and I was glad he was my friend! Clay had an amazing approach to problems (and it was the dot.com era, so we faced a ton), and I loved to watch him work. Our paths diverged, though, and we went our separate ways, losing touch as many former workmates do. In 2010 our paths crossed again, in a way I never imagined. Following the events of my dad's death, I had written and published a book that focused on his addiction, his death, and its effect on my life. Through the wonders of social media, I got a note from Clay one day that said something the to the effect of *"Mark, I never knew about the struggles with your dad … and you probably never knew that I, too, am an alcoholic..."* We reconnected, talked at length, and shared our stories with each other. And I could tell then that Clay had a gift for helping others in similar circumstances. I remember saying to him, *"If you could have spoken to my dad 10 years ago … he would be alive today!"* And I am so proud and excited to see that with *Beyond the Bottle* Clay is doing just that ... he's helping dads and mothers, husbands and wives, daughters and sons … you and me! Clay did not know it until later, but the conversations he and I had about addiction planted the seeds that prepared me for my wave in May of 2013. Through this book, Clay offers such practical advice and guidance from the perspective of someone who has fought and continues to fight the same battle. He is an incredible player-coach, and I know he can make a difference!

I encourage you to approach this book not as a book. Don't just read it and log it away in your mind. Approach it for what it is ... a lifesaver – for you, for someone you love, and put in the effort to change your life today. It is not by accident that you are holding this book in your hands right now, and one day you may look back and realize how significant this moment is. And recognize that the changes you make today aren't just for you … you hold in your hands the power to change your family tree forever ... and that's a mighty long time.

God bless and my prayers to you for your strength.

Mark McKinney is the author of "Faith on a Sticky Note" which chronicles the death of his father as a result of alcoholism. More importantly, though, Mark and I are great friends who have been brought closer by addiction and have strengthened each other through it all. Mark lives in Lincolnton, Georgia with his wife and two children.

Mark McKinney

http://www.faithonastickynote.com

CLAY CUTTS

INTRODUCTION

Quitting drinking and drugging is easy! All you have to do is…stop. For many of us, the hard part is *staying* quit. The REALLY hard part is learning how to live a fabulous life. After all, your goal is (or should be) to become the best possible version of yourself.

That's exactly what I do…help people overcome whatever their barriers might be in order to live a life full of joy and freedom. As a therapist I help people understand the emotional, behavioral, spiritual and intellectual "blind spots" that are keeping them from achieving their innate greatness.

I spent much of my life learning how to help people suffering from addictive diseases. Part of that learning has been "school-of-hard-knocks" type of education. But I also have the formal education that helps me take my game to the next level. I hold an undergraduate degree in Psychology and a Master's Degree in Social Work. Also, I'm a licensed therapist

This learning has allowed me the honor of working with addicted people in a variety of settings.

I am blessed to be on the staff of one of the premier substance abuse treatment facilities in the country. I work with professional men and women who find themselves struggling with addictions. My patients include physicians, pilots, veterinarians, nurses, dentists, entrepreneurs, executives and attorneys. Oh, and we help "normal people" too.

My private practice allows me to be of service to a slightly different population. I coordinate services with local Psychiatrists and Primary Care Physicians to provide mental health and behavioral interventions. Most of these clients have addiction issues. But many have other types of challenges as well…Anxiety Disorders, Depression, a history of trauma, unresolved grief issues, or simply difficult life circumstances.

In my "spare time" I work with local legal jurisdictions. I have been chosen to assess applicants who have found themselves in trouble with the law (typically following felony arrests) and make clinical recommendations for appropriate therapeutic interventions.

In my experience, even the most troubled individual has value. Addiction has obscured that value in many of my clients. Mistakes become the yardstick by which their life is measured. Removing alcohol and drugs is the first step. Building new, healthy, behaviors then becomes the real work of recovery.

In Beyond the Bottle: 9 Powerful Strategies to Reclaim Your Life, you will learn why addiction is a family disease. You will learn to see yourself as a person with a specific set of difficulties rather than as someone who is fundamentally flawed. You will learn practical exercises that will begin the process of healing. You will learn to see yourself accurately by recognizing your maladaptive patterns. You will learn how to have fun in sobriety and how to be a blessing to the people around you.

Most importantly, you will learn that you are not alone.

If I can get clean and sober, you can too!

BEYOND THE BOTTLE

CHAPTER 1: FIRST THINGS FIRST…

I loved alcohol. I loved everything about it…the smell, the taste, and most importantly, the way it made me feel.

There…I said it out loud!

Unfortunately, that love affair was doomed from the beginning. As much as I loved alcohol, the feelings were never reciprocated. Instead of allowing me to be the smart, funny, sexy guy I thought I was when I drank alcohol, it really made me into a fool. I became "that guy" people talked about the day after a party. Eventually I became the guy who didn't get invited to parties because I always made an ass out of myself. Actually, I think it's more accurate (and gentler on my tender ego) to say alcohol made an ass out of me.

Eventually I had to make a decision. Was I going to be a drinker or not? Now, just so you don't get the wrong idea, I didn't arrive at this decision point quickly or without considerable pain. I tried every trick I could think of to continue my unrequited love affair with the fair alcohol.

Despite my best efforts, and considerable creativity, I could not figure out a way to keep drinking AND maintain other parts of my life. For example, I needed to keep my job and wanted to keep my family. While I hadn't suffered any losses in those areas, they were clearly in jeopardy. Not to mention that my health and mental stability, such that they were, seemed in danger of vanishing as well.

So there I was…deciding whether to turn left or right. Would I be a drinker, with all the accompanying benefits, or a sober person, with that set of rewards?

For me the choice was clear. I made the decision, though with trepidation, to stop drinking. Like many others who came before me, I knew I couldn't do it alone since I had tried so many times before. If you are reading this book you may be in the same shoes I was in a few years back. You may need to decide which road to take…left or right.

Alcohol or Drugs?

Now I struggled specifically with alcohol. I experimented with some other drugs, but booze was the dragon that knocked me off my horse. Throughout this book sometimes I talk about drinking and sometimes I talk about drugs. It's important to understand that no matter what term I use, I'm talking about **your** drug of choice. So if you struggle with cocaine and I talk about alcohol, simply substitute "cocaine" whenever you read the word "alcohol."

The techniques I teach are applicable to any addiction, not just alcohol. It's just easier for me to write (and for you to read) "drinking" instead of "drinking and/or drugging." Addiction lives in the brain and is driven by the same mechanisms no matter what the specific substance might be. But that's a discussion for another time.

Should I Quit Drinking Right Away?

Right now the question is, should you should quit drinking right now? Or, even better, do you need to quit drinking in order to benefit from this book? The answer is…I can't answer that for you.

You have to decide on your own.

That said, I'll try to share some information that should make the decision easier. Just a few minutes ago I told you all addiction is the same. Well, I'm going to insert a footnote into that statement (already). It's important to understand that all chemicals affect the brain similarly. However, your withdrawal symptoms are likely to be different based on the specific drugs you have been using.

Generally speaking (very generally), your withdrawal is likely to make you feel the opposite of how your drug of choice made you feel. So, if you used a stimulant of some sort (maybe cocaine or methamphetamine), you are likely to encounter significant fatigue and depression. You might sleep for two or three days. Alternatively, if you used a central nervous system depressant such as alcohol, you may encounter agitation and insomnia when you quit.

Two classes of drugs require special attention. **This is important so please pay attention.** Seriously, you could die if you mess this up....

Opiate (pain pills and heroin) withdrawal is physically excruciating. The list of symptoms is nasty and as long as my arm. Suffice it to say you will feel like you got run over by a freight train.

Alcohol withdrawal can result in death. If you have been drinking heavily for a long time, quitting suddenly can literally be deadly. You run the risk of developing delirium tremens (a severe form of alcohol withdrawal with many nasty physical and emotional symptoms), going into seizures, or having a stroke.

So, no matter what your drug of choice, please get a physical before starting any substance abuse treatment program. At the very least have your blood pressure checked. I'm not just saying that because the lawyers said I must. In my private practice I routinely route new clients to the doctor before their first session. Many clients benefit from a medical detoxification in a hospital setting. This is nothing more than a day or two in a hospital bed with doctors and nurses monitoring your vital signs and treating individual symptoms (nausea, cramps, etc.). If you have been a heavy user, especially of opiates or alcohol, for a long time, please consider a two- or three-day detox.

Will Power or Real Power?

Will power is a myth. Okay, it's a real thing but it's just not very useful. Here's how will power works. I decide I'm going to stop eating sweets. I start off the day strong by eating a good, healthy breakfast. I occupy myself all day with work and other responsibilities. By the time I have my evening meal I'm tired and hungry. After dinner I wash dishes and help with homework and bath time for the kiddos.

Finally I sit down on the sofa with my wife, mentally and physically pooped. Any will power I had earlier in the day when I was well rested has been used up. So when my wife asks, with only love in her heart, if I want a bowl of ice cream I say…of course I do.

Will power is useful, but only up to a point.

When you are trying to change your lifestyle in significant ways will power will get you started, but it <u>will</u> fail you. When it does, you need something else. That "something else" is what this book is all about. Following the exercises here will allow you to create **Real Power** to change your life in a meaningful way.

Who Is This Book For?

Asking for help is hard. Even if you can screw up the courage to ask for help, how do you actually do it? Who do you ask? What do you say? It's easy for some well-meaning person to say, "That guy really should get some help with his drinking." Great…how, exactly, does that work?

For some people, walking into an AA or NA room and raising their hand is all that's necessary to start a sober life. For others, their faith tradition is the key to their recovery. Some people find the help they need from a private therapist or a traditional substance abuse program.

Each of these routes is valid and many addiction sufferers have used them with great success. If some combination of these treatment options works for you, great…more power to you. Consider yourself a lucky person! But what do you do if none of these methods work for you? Well, you try something else.

This book is not for everyone. I wish I could write a book that would solve every addiction issue for every person who ever struggled with substance use problems. Sorry…I'm not nearly that smart!

But I can write a book that helps a smaller sub-set of that population. The contents of this modest tome should be helpful to three distinct groups.

Group 1: People who are struggling with drugs or alcohol and want to quit.

If you are currently drinking or drugging and you think you may have a problem, this book was written specifically for you! You might have come to the realization that your life has begun to get off-track, or someone else might have pointed it out to you. Either way, reading this book is a great way to begin your sober journey.

Likewise, if you have come to understand your chemical use as a clear problem in your life and you've already taken the huge step of quitting, you are definitely in the right place.

Group 2: People who have been sober for a while but want to jumpstart their sobriety and take it to a new level.

Another important group who might find this book useful are those who have already been sober for a while, but who still feel like they could get more from a sober lifestyle than what they are getting. Very often, we get clean and sober due to external pressure. Your spouse or boss may give you an ultimatum, "Quit or else...." So, you quit and everyone is happy. Only...you're not happy.

You might relax a bit because the pressure is off.

To be clear, your life IS better. But you can't escape that subtle feeling way down in your gut that you're leaving something on the table. You may think, "I'm not drinking anymore, but I'm really not moving forward in other parts of my life."

If you have any of these feelings or you just want to put your sobriety in high gear, you are in the right place!

Group 3: People who have loved ones who are struggling with addictions.

Describing addiction as a family disease has become somewhat cliché. Nevertheless, watching someone you love repeatedly sabotage themselves through their behavior is heartbreaking. You wonder, "Why can't they just stop?" You watch with horror as they destroy their life one drink or one pill or one snort at a time. Yes, the effects of addiction spread way beyond the individual who is actually using the drugs or alcohol.

If someone you love is struggling with addiction, this book should impart hope in you and help you understand how someone might recover. Use this book as a source of insight into the mind of an addict, but also consider working through the exercises yourself. These tools are not specific to addiction. They are useful in learning to live a well-balanced life.

How to Use This Book

This book can be used either of two ways. If you would like, simply sit down and read through it from cover to cover. But please make use of the resources on the accompanying website. Hopefully you will find that you can get through the content fairly quickly. This is intentional since I would rather see you taking action toward your sobriety than to listen to me run my mouth.

Alternatively, you can use this book more like a workbook. You can, for example, read a chapter per day. As you read each chapter, you commit to doing the exercises described in that chapter. So in just over a week you will have built a repeatable routine that can become the foundation for your recovery plan.

However you use this book, please take the exercises seriously. Don't just read about them and say, "Oh that's nice," and move on. Pause long enough to work through the exercises. When people say, "Getting sober requires work," this is what they are talking about. Exercises like these are the beginning pieces of the work of sobriety.

<u>My Promise to You</u>

Yes, getting sober is hard. And sometimes I'll ask you to step way out of your comfort zone. Nobody wants to do that…I get it. But, that's where growth happens. So I'm asking for something I hope to earn: your trust. Dare to trust me and I'll do my best to help you move your life forward.

And I make you this promise…I will never ask you to put down something you are comfortable with unless I also teach you how to replace it with something even better. That's a promise!

CHAPTER 2: ACTION!

"Who is that guy?" I wondered as I looked in the mirror.

In my mind I was young and robust. The person looking back at me from my bathroom mirror was weathered and weary. His eyes were sunken and surrounded by dark rings. His face was puffy and pale. He looked…unwell.

On that October morning I was 35 years old, but I looked 60!

Standing at the bathroom vanity that morning I searched through the events of the previous evening, trying to piece it together. Though the details were vague, the theme was clear enough. It was familiar because it was the same story as most nights…plan to drink a little but end up drinking a lot and doing something dumb.

The reason for my sorry state was no mystery. Almost 20 years of hard drinking takes a serious toll on a body and on a mind. It all started off harmlessly enough. One steamy summer evening I was hanging out at a friend's house. We were 15 years old and bored. My buddy finally said, "Hey, I've got something you might like," and pulled out a bottle of whiskey.

He poured each of us a shot in a plastic cup and handed them out. Taking a deep breath, he drank his down then took a long slug from a 7-Up. He shook his head and looked at me as if to say, "Your turn." Bracing myself for the unexpected, I gulped the innocent-looking brown liquor. The taste didn't hit me immediately. A moment passed before the brunt of the wretchedness became manifest. It was terrible! My throat began to close and my eyes watered. My stomach started performing impossible gymnastic maneuvers. Mustering heroic willpower, I held back the vomit that was surely only moments away.

"How can people drink this crap?" I wondered

aloud.

My friend laughed and asked, "Do you want another?"

Pausing only momentarily I replied, "Yes."

After a third drink the liquor hit me. I somehow knew intuitively not to drink more lest I became sick. I had certainly seen my dad and other adults who had drank too much. I didn't want that. That night I achieved the perfect buzz.

That night everything changed for me. The awkward kid who was afraid of girls was gone. The boy who never quite fit in was now the life of the party. I was fundamentally different with a belly full of liquor…and I LOVED it!

That's how it all began for me. It was just a couple of bored guys hanging out in a basement experimenting with whiskey. That night was the beginning of an exciting journey. That journey would have some great times and some terrible times.

For the next 20 years drinking would be part of my life. It would be part of my identity. Alcohol was my constant companion and best friend. But at some point I crossed the invisible barrier between "wanting" to drink and "needing" to drink. Was it six months ago? Was it six years ago? That question would never be answered for me. The reality of that morning in my bathroom staring into the mirror was that I was trapped in the painful loop of hopelessness and despair that defines addiction. With all earnestness I swore off alcohol forever, knowing even as I spoke the words that I would be drunk again before I laid my head on the pillow that night.

Today my story is different. Do I live in a universe full of butterflies and rainbows? Of course not! I have the difficulties and challenges that accompany any busy life. My current reality differs from the life that caused me to not recognize myself in the mirror, though. Today I don't drink. In fact, I live my life without the interference of mind-altering chemicals of any kind.

So…how did I evolve from a broken man who was enslaved by alcohol to the new, free version of myself? I didn't become an alcoholic overnight. Likewise, I didn't heal from the effects of decades of drinking quickly. But one important variable stands out as the key to successful, long-term sobriety.

That key is ACTION. Nothing changes until something changes!

I tried to quit drinking many (many) times. Quitting seemed like an intellectual problem to be solved. "If I can just figure out *why* I drink I'll be able to control it or stop altogether." Specific types of booze became suspect as the culprits for my struggles with alcohol. Maybe I could stay away from brown liquor. Perhaps I should only drink beer or only drink wine? Even the timing of my drinking seemed to be the center of the problem. Alcoholics drink all day so I'll only drink after 6 p.m.

None of that worked!

At the time I was baffled since every idea I hatched seemed brilliant in my liquor-soaked brain. The truth is I was working on the wrong problem. Or at least I was working on the right problem in a very wrong way.

Instead of asking myself why I drank, I should have been asking myself why I wanted to be sober. Making a big change in my life required a big effort, and the energy to bring forth that big effort required a big "WHY" behind it. In other words, if I was going to get sober I needed to have a hugely powerful reason to do it. Until my why got big enough, I was just going to flounder around and make myself crazy. I was going to struggle in my life. I was going to stay drunk!

If, like me, drugs and/or alcohol are holding you back and you want to change…your why needs to be a **WHY** if you are going to meet your goal of long-term sobriety. Your first challenge is to ask the right question. Why do you want to get clean and sober? If you don't have a really good answer to this question you may be able to quit drinking or using drugs, but high-quality, life-changing sobriety will likely remain elusive.

How do you nail down your WHY? I'm going to walk you through an exercise that will help you get to that answer.

Before we get started, discussing the importance of this exercise is critical. You see, most people with addictions issues will never make any attempt to get clean and sober. The sad truth is that the majority of addicts will die from their disease. We will never know the true numbers due to misdiagnosis and under-reporting based on lack of training in the medical field and the persistent stigma addiction still carries.

On the other hand, some people will make an effort to solve their drinking or drug problem. Those folks have a chance. Even among those who make an effort, many will fail. Some will eventually figure it out, but a heartbreaking number will eventually die from addiction.

I say this not to be dramatic or discouraging. On the contrary, I want to encourage you to do the one thing that all successful people do. I want to encourage you to take bold action. This exercise is important because it will represent your first opportunity to make a change. It will be your first crossroads.

Will you put down this book and do the exercise? Will you take immediate, decisive action, or will you dismiss my warnings and plow ahead? I know…you say you'll come back later and do the exercises. I believe that you believe that. But I know from experience that folks, even those with the best of intentions, never come back and finish the exercises.

Nobody ever got sober from reading about recovery, any more than they got in shape from reading about pushups!

Exercise: "The Perfect Day"

The Perfect Day exercise is a tool you can use to help create a huge WHY in your mind. It will let you see, with clarity, what your life could be like. Then you can decide if that picture in your mind is worth working for. "Working" is the important word here because, make no mistake, conquering addiction requires work.

This exercise requires some writing, so grab a pen and a notebook. Seriously, stop reading and get some paper and something to write with. Remember, nothing changes until you do something different. That means taking action.

Write down the details of how you would spend your perfect day if drugs and/or alcohol were not holding you back. For example, I've worked with many people who have lost the right to spend time with their children due to their addictive behavior. Their perfect day would likely involve activities with their kids. Your perfect day is probably different, but experience has shown me that people who suffer from addictive problems always miss out on something due to their drinking or drug use.

The truth is that the disease of addiction wants to take everything from you. It wants you broke, lonely, isolated, depressed and, eventually, dead. This is why focusing on the positive version of your life, the version without drugs or alcohol, is critically important.

Now that you have your tools and you have a basic understanding of why we are doing this exercise, let's begin. At the top of the page, write "My Perfect Day" or something similar. Also add today's date. I always like to date whatever I'm working on so I can look back later and say, "Man…I was brilliant on that day!"

You can do this however you like, but here are some questions you can use to prompt your writing. What time of year is it? What is the weather like? Who are you with (or are you alone)? Do you wake up early or sleep in? What meals do you have? Are they eaten at home or at a restaurant? What do you do? Where do you go? Do you focus on one fun hobby all day or do you try several new activities?

This exercise has one more component that is, arguably, much harder than the part you just completed. As you might expect, it's also more valuable. After all, high effort and difficulty often leads to more valuable outcomes, right?

After you have a snapshot of your perfect day

that includes answers to the where, when, who, how and what types of questions, it's time to think about the emotions involved. How will you feel as you go through this day? Will you be excited or scared? Will you feel grateful? I can only guess how you will be feeling based on my experiences, but my wish is that at least one of the emotions you experience is hope!

None of this has to be written in complete sentences. You can just write phrases or fragments or even single words. Write it any way you like, as long as it's something you understand. Also, feel free to suspend reality. The idea is to open your mind and let you see beyond your current circumstance. For example, you may want to have a croissant and coffee for breakfast in Paris, then have your mother's home-cooked meatloaf for lunch in Albuquerque.

Don't be afraid to invest some time in this activity. Don't just throw it together and move on. The idea is to create a believable image in your mind's eye of how your life could be. This picture needs to be crystal clear and desirable to you. If this image is pleasant enough and powerful enough and fills you with enough hope, you can use it as your WHY. When you get frustrated or are on the verge of relapse, this big WHY will be an important tool to keep you safe.

Now, I enjoy writing and think in terms of text, but I know not everyone does. So feel free to let your creative juices flow and play to your strengths. Maybe you can draw a series of pictures that illustrate your perfect day. Maybe you could write a song about it. The important part is to create something important to you! Create something that stirs your emotions and makes you want to reach out and grab it.

Whatever you create, put it somewhere safe. This will be an important tool to pull out later in your sobriety journey. Now let's look at another exercise that will help you get ready to move forward in a big way.

Exercise: "The Willingness Workout"

Willingness is a fundamental principle in any activity designed to make changes in your life. I often use fitness as an example because most people can relate to the difficulty of staying on an exercise regimen for an extended period of time. Simply committing to a new lifestyle in your mind can be challenging enough. The really hard part is staying focused and motivated for the middle and long term. Unfortunately, we don't enjoy most of the valuable outcomes until further along.

In my experience working with people in private practice I can often anticipate an individual client's future level of success. Now, I'm surprised both positively and negatively fairly often. But I guess correctly pretty often as well.

The one variable that always (and I don't use that word often) sways the scale is the degree to which they are willing to do "whatever it takes" to achieve their goals. A man or woman who gets to that point of willingness is absolutely unstoppable. I could literally build a cinderblock wall in their path and they will either climb over it or smash their way through it to get to their goal.

If a client does not have that high level of willingness that I know leads to success, I typically slow down and make sure to address their low willingness. The first step is to gauge their initial level of willingness on a scale of 0 to 100. A willingness level of 0 means you have absolutely no intention of making any changes at all. Further, you refuse to see any room for improvement in yourself or in your current circumstances. Frankly, I doubt many readers of this book fall at this end of the spectrum. The very act of buying and reading this material is an act of willingness.

In fact, if you have read to this point, take a minute and congratulate yourself. It may not seem like much of a victory to you yet, but I think it's significant. This reminds me of an old question…how do you eat an elephant? The answer is simple: you eat him one bite at a time. Likewise, you don't get sober all at once. You get sober one small victory and one small step at a time.

On the other end of the willingness scale is 100. Folks who judge themselves as being at this level are highly motivated. They are also rare. If they have a drinking or drug problem, they may be able to completely abstain just on the sheer force of their will. This level of commitment is fantastic. But even these folks should seek some help in their recovery journey. I can think of two reasons for not trying to get sober alone, even for highly willing individuals. First, willingness levels change from day to day and from hour to hour. Having a relationship with someone who can help you is critically important when your willingness or motivation wanes. Second, true long-term sobriety with all its many rewards is very different from simple abstinence. Getting clean and sober is likely a new undertaking for you, and wise guidance is good idea if you are going to get the most out of your efforts.

It's time to decide where you are on the motivation scale. The question is, on a scale of 0 to 100, how willing are you to do *whatever it takes* to get clean and sober? My suggestion would be to write down that question and the answer.

If your willingness score is over 80, then you should consider yourself on track for success. Don't rest on your laurels, though. Willingness can ebb from day to day. If your willingness score was less than 80, we have some work to do. Don't panic! Just know that willingness is an area where you are going to need to focus as we move forward. The exercises in the rest of this book are designed to exercise your willingness muscles.

I've had the honor of working with men and women who have found themselves in a substance abuse treatment setting after running afoul of the law. To say most of these folks lacked willingness is like saying the desert lacks water: a huge understatement. One client stands out in my mind as being especially focused in her desire to be anywhere but in a therapy room. She wasn't overtly rude, but her disdain for the process was written on her face.

The Story of Alice

Alice was sent to me by the court system after earning her third DUI. During our first session she sat across from me with her arms crossed. She stared at a spot on the wall about three feet to my right. As I engaged her in conversation, she rolled her eyes. In fact, she rolled them so far I was worried they were going to roll right out of her head. Everything about her screamed, "I DON'T WANT TO BE HERE!"

But she had to be there. And eventually she realized she needed to be there. As we worked together, something changed in her. She became less oppositional and stopped fighting the clinical staff and the recovery process. She became willing to do the work. As soon as she turned that corner, her entire outlook changed and recovering actually became fun for her.

Hearing from clients after treatment ends is unusual. So, several months later when I got an email from this client, it really stood out. In her email she described a life that was finally on track. She was free of addiction, on a career track that truly suited her, and had accomplished several other important goals. I take no credit for her success. She is winning because she was willing to take a huge risk and do whatever it took to get her life back.

This client won and you can too.

I get it…this can be terrifying. At the very least you likely feel anxious about making such a significant life change. You may also experience some anger at not being able to drink or use your drug of choice. A part of you may also feel optimistic about the possibility of living a better life.

Be bold, take ACTION and do the work! Speaking of being bold, don't just read these words and file them away in the back of your mind. Check in with the author for a message on taking bold action…http://sergeantsober.com/link1/.

Invest in yourself and your future by doing the exercises in this book. Don't let another day (or week or month or year) pass without standing up for yourself and your family. Don't look in the mirror one more time and wonder how you became that person staring back with hollow eyes. You can do it…I believe in you.

Chapter 2 Action Steps:
1. Complete the "Perfect Day" exercise.
2. Complete the "Willingness Workout" exercise.

CHAPTER 3: BROADEN YOUR VISION!

I'm like the guy who buys a baby tiger from a shady dealer in a dark alley. The little cat is just so cute, how could I resist? At first he just drinks milk…a lot of it. As he grows, he starts eating meat. He grows and grows, but he's still cute. But as he gets bigger and stronger, something about him sets me on edge. I begin to realize, mostly on a subconscious level, that my pet is dangerous. Eventually he gets so big and strong that I can't control him. All I can do is hang on for the ride and hope for the best.

I may be able to deal with him for years (or even decades), but if I don't do something about this wild animal living with me, he will likely eventually kill me. And he won't do it because he's evil or because he hates me. He will do it because it's in his nature.

My addiction is just like that tiger. It starts off as harmless but it eventually grows fangs and claws. If I'm not careful, it will rip my head off.

Just like the tiger, your addiction will allow you to feed it and pet it for a while. But eventually the relationship will change because, in the end, the disease of addiction wants everything from you! It is not good at sharing or compromising. Like the tiger, addiction isn't necessarily good or evil. It doesn't take from you for enjoyment or sport. It simply behaves in a manner consistent with its nature. *Addiction* is not happy until it steals everything valuable you ever had. For some people that means literally losing everything. Recently I was working with a client, "Andy," who was in jail. He had been a hardworking, independent, self-sufficient member of society. Andy had supported his family and "taken care of business" for years. That all changed when he turned to drugs following a traumatic life event. Today he literally does not have a single possession to his name.

That's how addiction wants you: broken and helpless.

After years of drinking and drugging you might not be the same person. Even if you didn't lose everything like Andy, you might have lost sight of who you are and what you value.

The Story of "Mike"

"Mike" has been living a sober life since giving up alcohol over 20 years ago. He told me this story....

"In my drinking days I hurt my wife, stole from every employer I ever had, pushed away my friends, took advantage of my parents and lied to everyone I met. Even with all that going for me I still thought I was a pretty good person. I honestly thought alcohol was my ONLY problem. When I looked inside at how miserable I was I just knew that if I could only, somehow, quit drinking, everything would be fine.

"Well, it turns out that I had a lot more problems than just alcohol. Mostly I was angry. I was angry with myself and with everyone around me. I was even angry with God. Early on I realized that drinking and drugging took the edge off my anger. Eventually I got to the point that I couldn't quit drinking or drugging, which made me mad at myself! I was just a walking time bomb. Hurting myself or someone else was just a matter of time.

"I saw myself as broken and flawed in every way. At the same time, my expectations for myself were insanely high. I

thought I had to be perfect, but saw myself as a total loser. The truth is that I was just a guy, imperfect by design, who was doing the best he could do. Today I definitely don't do anything perfectly. But I can honestly say that my worst day now is WAY better than my best day when I was in active addiction. It's taken a lot of years to fix the broken parts of me, but I'm happy to have made the effort."

This is an incredibly common story in recovery circles. Abusing drugs or alcohol for years can blur your identity and obscure your place in the world. An important part of recovering from addiction is to bring your vision back into focus. The exercises in this chapter are designed to do exactly that. They are built to sharpen your vision and help you look at yourself and get a clear image of who you really are.

Now, this may be scary, especially if you are carrying around guilt about how you conducted your life when you were actively drinking or using drugs. And make no mistake…most people get to this point carrying some bad feelings about themselves and others. Clarifying and broadening your vision are important because having that accurate picture of yourself gives you a starting point for your recovery journey.

We are going to talk about three techniques for fixing your broken perception of who you were, who you are, and who you might be in the future. These techniques are the Motion Board exercise, Journaling, and Quiet Time.

Exercise: "Motion Board"

For years, teachers in the self-improvement and motivation space have advocated creating "vision boards." A vision board is a tool that helps clarify what you are working toward. Like the "Perfect Day" exercise from the previous chapter, it allows you to bring a future reality into focus. The idea of a vision board is to find pictures of items from magazines, newspapers or online that represent your future. For example, you may have a picture of a beach with palm trees on your vision board because part of your dream is to go on a tropical vacation.

Vision boards are useful, but they can miss the point. For example, I've seen people put pictures of mansions and very expensive cars on their boards. I believe all things are possible, and I believe that, given enough effort, you could acquire those items. But my question is this: is that what you REALLY want?

Instead of vision boards, I think people should create Motion Boards. They are similar to vision boards in that they still provide you with a highly focused image of what you want your life to look like. However, Motion Boards have one very important rule: you can only include items on the board if you are 100 percent committed to moving toward that item *today*.

STRATEGY 1: JOURNALING

I don't know about you but I live a busy life. My attention is pulled in a thousand different directions all day. Sometimes I get overwhelmed to the point that thoughts, ideas and worries bounce around in my head like a tipped-over box of ping-pong balls. This is not a healthy way to live, so I try to quiet my mind as quickly as possible. The best method I have found is journaling.

You are probably in one of three schools of thought when it comes to journaling. You may think that keeping a journal is the domain of 13-year-old, boy-crazy, hormonally overloaded girls. You may have never thought of journaling as being related in any way to your emotional health. Or you may already be a dedicated journaler.

Let's start off by being clear that when I talk about journaling I'm not talking about the "dear diary" sort of stuff you might find hidden under your daughter's pillow. I'm not talking about recording every emotional flight of fancy that crosses your mind.

I'm talking about using a powerful tool, in a purposeful way, to clarify your thoughts and allow you to focus on the areas of your life that need attention. Something magical happens when you put your thoughts into writing. I'm going to help you add that trick to your bag.

Why Journal?

Journaling has some clear positive implications for your overall health. Putting your thoughts in writing is good for your emotional well-being. A 2011 study (Utley & Garza, 2011) found the use of journaling "can lead to a greater self-awareness and growth." Of course, keeping a journal is not new. Politicians, soldiers, explorers, scientists and normal people have been keeping journals (or diaries or logs or ledgers) since ancient Roman times.

Journaling is also good for your physical health. "Keeping one's thoughts and feelings inside can be stress producing. By lowering the stress level, the individual's immune system functions better" (Landis, 2004).

One study even found that holistic interventions such as journaling can be useful in treating serious mental health issues such as generalized anxiety disorder (McPherson & McGraw, 2013).

If you have always thought of journaling as something for other people or that could never help you, I encourage you to open your mind. Sometimes when we expand our mind and consider the impossible, amazing change happens.

How to Journal

The most important rule of journaling is to just get started. The second most important rule is to not make it complicated. Journaling is truly as simple as getting a notebook and a pen and starting writing.

Sara Rowe (2012) recommends some journaling prompts that will help you get started. A few of these prompts are: "Today I…"; "I remember when…"; "I'm most worried about…"; and "Something about myself I would like to change…." Of course, these are just suggestions. Feel free to come up with dozens of your own.

Another name for the prompts described by Rowe is "sentence stem." The term has been around for a long time, but I learned it from a man named Rich Schefren. Using sentence stems is really easy. It's one of those easy activities that seem unnatural at first. But, if you persist for just a little while, I promise that you will understand sentence stems for the incredibly powerful tool they really are.

Start with a sentence stem you find somewhere, such as those suggested above by Rowe, or by making up your own. Let's work through an example.

Let's imagine I notice I've been feeling out of sorts lately. I seem to have been plagued by a general worry, but can't quite put my finger on what I'm worried about. Maybe I'm having trouble concentrating. Perhaps I'm struggling to get to sleep at night. I might start with a sentence stem from above such as "I'm most worried about...." I would write that stem on my journal page. I would then come up with three or four possible responses.

I may write the following:

"...a big project coming up at work."
"...communication problems with my spouse."
"...my child's recent behavior problems at school."
"...health concerns with my aging mother and father."

Of course, your responses will be your own depending on what's going on in your life. In fact, worry may not even be an issue for you. But in this example you can see that I may be worried about several unrelated items.

The idea is to use the same sentence stem every day and add three or four new responses each day. You can add responses for a few days or for several weeks. Each day, try to add unique responses without looking at the responses from the previous day. Eventually some patterns will start to arise among the responses. In my experience, those patterns pop out pretty quickly. I'm amazed at the clarity that develops in my thinking every time I use this technique. You can use this to work out all sorts of issues: thinking errors, business problems, relationship challenges…the list is nearly endless.

Taking Action!

As an eighteen-year-old college freshman I was bulletproof and had the answer to everything. I thought I had everything figured out and that nobody had anything to teach me. A professor in a creative writing class was talking to us about the importance of "just writing." She was saying that we often overthink what we want to write to the point that we don't write anything at all.

Her assignment was for us to get out a paper and pen and just start writing. Of course I thought the assignment was ridiculous since I was clearly smarter than this very accomplished Ph.D. level professor.

At the time I was on a big Beatles kick, so I started writing my story something like this: "I'm being forced to write a story without giving it much thought. I don't have anything to write about but I don't want to be the one guy in the class just staring into space, so I'm writing this nonsense. I'll bet when Paul McCartney wrote 'Let It Be' he didn't just sit down at the piano and say, 'Today I'm going to write a really great song today.' No, I don't think it happened that way."

I then went on to write a decent fictional story about how Paul McCartney came up with, and then composed, "Let It Be." Several years later I found the story and almost vomited at how sappy it was. But that little story served its purpose. It (and the wise teacher, of course) showed me that sometimes the best way to write is to just write.

So I challenge you to pick up pen and paper...and just write!

Strategy 2: QUIET TIME

Another ancient but incredibly effective method for quieting your mind and regaining focus is meditation, which I refer to as "Quiet Time." You may be picturing a monk with a shaved head sitting in a lotus position for six hours when you think of meditation. Yes, that's certainly one aspect of meditation. But I think of meditation from a different perspective.

Try not to get bogged down in the details or terminology. One practice shared by many successful people in history is meditation. They may have called it that, or referred to it as prayer, mindfulness, or any of a number of terms. Depending on the purpose of the exercise, the activity may differ. For example, if you think of this time as prayer, you may speak to the god of your understanding. If you think of this as meditation, you may focus on a key word such as "peace" or "serenity." If you think of this time as mindfulness, you may focus on your current state to the exclusion of the past or present.

As you can see, significant variation exists even within the narrow scope of the act of sitting quietly. Therefore I label this practice simply as Quiet Time.

When I say Quiet Time, feel free to substitute whatever term makes the most sense to you. If you would like to pray, do so. If you would rather focus on your breathing, that's fine. Simply being still and trying to clear your mind is perfectly acceptable as well.

Before we get into the details of the "how," let's look at the "why." In short, practices such as meditation will help keep you sober. According to a 2007 article in the journal of the American Counseling Association, "Successful addiction recovery is often related to an individual's ability to develop and use a repertoire of coping behaviors" (Pruett et al., 2007). Meditation is a prime example of one of these effective coping behaviors.

Addictive behavior is never just about drinking or using drugs. Other factors are always at play under the surface. Addiction can be seen as a "soul sickness." Many people who fall into the trap of drug use or excessive drinking have other issues that contribute. Now, I'm not saying that you became an alcoholic because your mommy didn't give you a rubber ducky or because your daddy didn't play catch with you enough. I am saying other psychosocial factors can be involved. As a therapist and addiction counselor, encountering clients with past traumas, unresolved grief, or mental health challenges (such as depression or anxiety) is incredibly common.

Whether these issues caused the drinking or not we will never know. But we do know that carrying around this "baggage" creates an unhealthy amount of noise in your head. This noise is often enough to hold you back from accomplishing your important life goals.

Why should you meditate? Woodham and Peters, as cited by Haynes and Zabel (2004), referred to meditation as "a state of heightened mental awareness and inner peace that brings mental, physical, and spiritual benefits. It is a useful self-help technique and can be practiced without adherence to any religion or philosophy" (p. 19).

So developing the habit of sitting quietly each day will gradually train your mind to turn down the internal volume. This will create room to learn new skills and focus on the positive changes you want to make.

The whole point of you taking this time each day is for you to get to know yourself again. After years (or maybe decades) of abusing your body and mind with chemicals, you likely have an inaccurate picture of who you are. Taking quiet time is a key tool in helping you become reacquainted with yourself. After all, you need to know who you are now if you are going to become something better in the future. And becoming the best possible version of you is the whole point!

How to Practice Quiet Time

Entire libraries could be filled on the topic of meditation. Duplicating that huge body of work is clearly outside the scope of our conversation here, so let's just keep this really simple. I'll just walk you through how I practice the Quiet Time exercise. You can feel free to follow my method or tweak it to suit your needs and beliefs.

I like to have my quiet time early in the morning before I begin my day. Sometimes I wake up with a to-do list running through my mind. If I can quiet that chatter and get focused before starting my hectic day, I am often much more productive.

When I wake up I go immediately into a small sitting room in our house. I plop down on an old leather sofa that my wife hates. (It's comfortable but has definitely seen better days.) When I'm settled, I grab one of the inspirational books I keep on the table beside the sofa. These books cover a variety of topics: recovery, business, philosophy, religion, etc. I am always looking for texts that speak to me on some level.

I then read for a brief period…maybe 10 or 15 minutes. Once I've taken in some nourishment for my brain, I put down the book and work on digestion. I close my eyes and focus on what I just read. Sometimes it's a passage from the Bible, so I focus on what lesson I can learn about my spiritual journey. Sometimes I've read from a business book, so I try to understand how that reading could apply to my business.

As a person of faith I also spend a few minutes chatting with God as I understand Him. If this doesn't fit your beliefs, feel free to skip this part. I have found that the universe possesses great power that is beyond my comprehension. A connectedness also exists and this quiet time seems to help me plug into this larger picture.

Your Progress So Far

At this point you may be feeling some annoyance or apprehension. These types of exercises might be new to you and you may not think such techniques will benefit you at all. On the other hand this new approach may pique your interest and allow you to feel some hope about the future. If you have just quit drinking or using drugs, you likely feel pretty lousy. You may be shaky and nauseated. You probably either feel like sleeping all the time (withdrawal from stimulants) or can't sleep at all (withdrawal from central nervous system depressants).

Try to not become too upset about any unpleasant physical or mental symptoms you may be experiencing. Try to take comfort in knowing you are right where you should be. You are walking the path that so many others have walked before you. Just focus on your goals and keep pushing forward. Know that a life of freedom, hope, serenity and sobriety is the pot of gold at the end of this particular rainbow.

Chapter 3 Action Steps:

1. Start working on your Motion Board. This will be an ongoing project to which you can add new ideas as they occur.
2. Create a journal and make your first entry. Don't over-think...just put pen to paper and write.
3. Spend some Quiet Time and become focused and centered.

CHAPTER 4: CLARIFY YOUR THINKING!

"But I don't want to be an alcoholic," I ranted.

The man across the table from me crossed his arms and sat back in his chair, clearly trying to swallow a laugh. "You don't **want** to be an alcoholic?"

"No," I said indignantly, "of course not. Who the hell wants to be an addict or alcoholic?"

"Well, me for one."

I stared at Joe, not sure if he was pulling my leg or being serious (it was always hard to tell with him). "You want to be an addict?"

"Well, I'm not sure I want to be an addict. Though what I want is pretty irrelevant. I can say that I've learned to be grateful for all my struggles, including those with drugs and alcohol. I see every challenge in my life as teaching me something useful or moving me forward in some way."

I continued to stare at him, unconvinced.

"Okay," he said patiently, "let me tell you another story that might help you understand what I'm saying." Joe sipped his coffee then reclined in his chair, clearly searching for a starting point for his story. "I was always a really hardworking guy. I took pride in the great job I did providing for my family. I traveled and worked late whenever the company needed me. And it was working out because I was really seen as the 'go-to' guy at work."

He continued, "Then one day I had a terrible pain in my chest. I was rushed to the hospital with a severe heart attack. It was touch and go for a while, but I pulled through, obviously. As I recovered, my wife and I spent a lot of time talking. That was about all I could do since I was so weak. As we spent time together it became clear that she had not been happy for a long time. In fact, she had been thinking about leaving me. She complained that I worked almost all the time, and that when I wasn't working I was drinking in order to recharge my batteries so I could work some more."

Joe paused, looking closely at me. "Do you hear what I'm telling you?"

Nodding my head in agreement I said, "I think so. It sounds like you're telling me to slow down and appreciate my relationships."

"Yeah, that's part of it. But more importantly, something really bad had to happen for me to change the course of my life. Now some people aren't as hardheaded as me. They can see a bad thing coming and get out of the way in time. For me, the collision had to occur. So, I now see one of the scariest times of my life as incredibly valuable. It's a matter of perspective. I'm only better now because my **thinking** is better!"

My wise friend Joe taught me about growth through better thinking, which leads us to a question: How do we grow? I'm not asking about how we become taller or wider. I'm talking about emotional growth and development. How do we become mature, well-adjusted adults?

The simple answer is that we grow by suffering. That may sound negative or even harsh. But if you think about it, we only grow when we are confronted with challenges we don't know how to handle. We figure it out. I love the quote by Neale Donald Walsch that says, "Life begins at the end of your comfort zone." This is definitely congruent with my experience.

In her 1969 book *On Death and Dying*, Elisabeth Kübler-Ross described five stages of mourning. She was specifically describing our reaction to the death of a loved one. However, these stages are relevant to any difficult situation.

The five stages are:

1. Denial – "This can't be happening"
2. Anger – "I'm so mad this is happening"
3. Bargaining – "I'll do anything to keep this from happening"
4. Depression – "I'm so sad this happened"
5. Acceptance – "Oh well, I guess it happened"

Let's look at a 16-year-old girl whose boyfriend breaks up with her. How does she respond? One option is for her to follow the stages of change described by Kübler-Ross. In this case our young lady would begin by saying something like, "You aren't really breaking up with me...I must have heard you wrong." Then she would get angry and say, "HOW DARE YOU BREAK UP WITH ME!" Later she would begin bargaining and say something like, "I'll do anything to keep you from breaking up with me." Her next stage would be depression where she would say, "I'm so sad that he broke up with me...I think I'll sleep all day." Eventually (especially if she had good support from friends and family), she would accept her situation by saying, "It's okay that he broke up with me...I'll meet the right person eventually."

That's how a healthy person responds to a difficult situation. Think of this young lady's predicament as her adding one more brick to the building that will eventually become her future mature, adult self. She will encounter other challenges in her life. If she continues to respond in healthy, though painful, ways she will keep adding bricks to her building, eventually becoming an emotionally stable adult.

However, she may take a different route. When Junior calls her (or more likely sends her a text) to break up with her, she will likely jump into the

Denial stage. However, she may have learned from her parents, friends, movies, television or elsewhere that a couple shots of vodka from her parents' liquor cabinet will take the edge off the pain. She may take that shot or smoke that bowl or pop that pill. Doing so will change her emotional state enough to prevent her from navigating the other stages. Importantly, she may never get to the Acceptance stage. Therefore, she misses an important opportunity to add a brick to her building.

If she does this once or twice she will likely develop normally. The danger is when dealing with life's challenges with chemicals becomes a habit.

A client, "Marty," explains this concept very well.

"My first drinks were beers stolen from my father's stash in the refrigerator in the basement. I was in maybe seventh or eighth grade. My buddies and I would grab a few beers then go hang out in the woods and have a great time. Three of us could get wasted on a six-pack in those days. When I got sober at 40 I noticed I had lots of trouble dealing with the normal stuff that happens in life. I would get crazy mad about the smallest things. Eventually I learned that I was basically a 40-year-old man acting like a 15-year-old boy. I spent all those years drinking over problems rather than

growing up like most other people."

Clearly, lack of emotional development is a big problem. But that lack of development actually has deeper ramifications. A lifetime of failing to deal with life as it happens actually "breaks" your thinking. The pattern works something like this...you encounter a problem, you get high or drunk, and when you sober up you feel remorse and guilt. As this pattern plays out, you may think of yourself in extreme terms. You may think of yourself as flawed or bad or "a loser" because you got drunk again when you didn't want to. Eventually your entire self-image may become skewed based on this flawed thinking. This pattern needs to be adjusted.

If you have trouble dealing with life's challenges or if you feel like you are missing something or you don't seem to think about things like others, don't worry. Most of us have been in that same situation. Hopefully the last couple of pages will help you understand a possible explanation for how you feel.

So...if you drank or used drugs during your formative years (or during any other large chunk of your life), does this mean you're out of luck? **Of course not!** I wouldn't bother to write this book if there was no hope. You will likely never become the person you would have become without those years of drinking or drugging. BUT…you can become a fantastic version of yourself. This may sound crazy right now, but I predict one day you will actually count your struggles with chemicals as a blessing. Overcoming that challenge will make you stronger than you could have ever become otherwise.

But how do you overcome all those missed years of emotional development? How do you fix your broken thinking? I recommend a couple of specific strategies. Both of them are designed to help you stop thinking of yourself in unrealistic ways. They will help you see yourself as a valuable person living in a fair and logical world. This type of thinking pushes away anxiety and depression symptoms. It also will bring peace and serenity into your life.

I call these two strategies "The Attitude Adjustment" and "The Gratitude Attitude."

Strategy 3: THE ATTITUDE ADJUSTMENT

If you think of yourself in an unrealistically negative way you will never be happy. That's pretty obvious. This exercise will help you see yourself accurately…not all good but not all bad. The idea is to get okay with just being okay.

It's time to get out a piece of paper or your journal. At the top write "My Qualities" or something that make sense to you. Remember to write the date on the page as well. You may want to look back at this in the future.

Write down what you see as you worst or most unflattering quality. If you can't think of anything, just ask your mother-in-law. She will give you a long list from which to choose. Seriously though, this may be a good time to enlist the help of your spouse or a close friend. Make sure the person you ask for help is someone you trust and who is supportive of the work you are doing here. Some people will not understand what you are trying to accomplish and will try to talk you out of changing.

Under the name of the quality, list some evidence of that quality in you. Try to list three to five points that prove the attribute really does describe you. For example, you may feel (or have been told) you are selfish. You would document this not-so-favorable trait like this:

Negative Quality: Selfishness

Evidence:

1. I tend to talk about myself and not ask others how their life is going.

2. When I see a mess in the house my first reaction is to hope someone else   cleans it up so I don't have to.

3. I usually don't let others in the group decide on activities we do.

This is a generic example, but I hope it helps you see that this doesn't have to be overcomplicated. Just keep two rules in mind. First, be honest. Second, actually write it down on paper.

The second part of this exercise is to document positive characteristics of your personality. Do the same as above except focus on something good. The other side of the coin for selfishness would be something like "thoughtful." The evidence for you as a thoughtful person would be that you look for ways to help others, make sure your family has their needs met before yours, and are open to compromising in a group.

I would encourage you to repeat the exercise for more than one positive quality. After years (or maybe decades) of drinking and/or drugging you may see yourself pretty negatively. Many people in early sobriety experience significant feelings of guilt, shame and remorse. Part of that is natural because you likely engaged in some behaviors you're not proud of. Another part of these feelings is related to changes in your brain caused by suddenly depriving it of chemicals.

The point is that you likely have an opinion of yourself that is not entirely accurate. Most recently sober men and women tend to beat themselves up unnecessarily. Hopefully this exercise will demonstrate that you likely have some not-so-great characteristics that could use some work, but that you also have some positive qualities on which you can build the rest of the new, sober you.

Strategy 4: THE GRATITUDE ATTITUDE

The next exercise is an oldie but a goodie. It's elegant in its simplicity. So much so that it likely gets overlooked for the powerful tool it really is. I'm talking about the "gratitude list."

A gratitude list is exactly what it sounds like: a list of things for which you are grateful. To create one, simply pull out your journal and write "Gratitude List" at the top of a blank page and start writing.

Most people tend to start out with the large,

obvious things and get more focused as they progress. For example, you may start your list with your health, your spouse, and your children. Those are important, but gratitude for smaller things is fine as well. For example, I live in a hot climate, but today is cool and crisp. I almost needed a jacket when I went outside this morning. I find myself being grateful for a rare but welcomed change in temperature.

The reason for gratitude is simple. We only have so much "emotional bandwidth" to spend at any given time. If we consume that bandwidth with negativity, self-loathing and un-helpful thoughts, we will be defined by this pessimistic, unfavorable reality. But, if we fill our thoughts and minds with positive thoughts and emotions such as gratitude, we have a tendency to lean to a more optimistic, favorable reality.

By the time you finish this mission, you will hopefully be experiencing some positive emotions such as optimism about your future and happiness about the progress you have made in the program. Unfortunately, you will probably still be fairly shaky. Hang in there…it will pass soon. You may also feel some resistance to these steps since they are likely out of your comfort zone. I encourage you to take a deep breath and push forward toward the extremely valuable goal of sobriety.

Sergeant Sober has a quick message for you... http://sergeantsober.com/link2/.

After so many years of beating yourself up for not being able to quit drinking and/or using drugs, you likely have an image of yourself that's not 100 percent accurate. The exercises in this chapter, especially if they are repeated regularly, will gradually help you see yourself clearly. You are not all good or all bad. You are okay...and that's okay.

Chapter 4 Action Steps:
1. Complete the "Positive Qualities" exercise.
2. Write your first "Gratitude List."

CHAPTER 5: HAVING FUN IN SOBRIETY

The golf cart made a sharp left turn and nearly tossed me out of the passenger seat. Shaking myself back to semi-consciousness, I grabbed the frame of the cart and held on for dear life. Glancing at the driver I saw two rows of teeth bared at me in a ridiculous smile.

"What hole is this?" I asked.

"We're finished, man," was the confusing reply.

I searched my memory, trying to fill in the blanks. We had been playing at our favorite golf course and drinking beer, like usual. At some point someone…maybe it was me…pulled out a bottle of vodka. I clearly remembered seeing a sign for the 12th hole. After that, the images became increasingly foggy.

Toward the end of my drinking career, that became the typical story of how a game of golf ended for me. I would start out with the intention of sipping a few beers with my buddies as we made our way around the course. But, invariably, I would drink too much and either pass out, black out, or just get too drunk to play.

Drinking was gradually taking everything from me. It was even stealing my favorite pastime. After decades of playing golf, it wasn't even fun anymore.

Can you guess the single most common question I'm asked? I'll bet you can because you've probably asked it yourself. Even if you haven't said it out loud, I'll bet you've thought it. The question is, "If I quit drinking/drugging, what will I do with my time? I don't want to become some boring person who never does anything interesting."

Am I right? Have you wondered that?

I know I asked that question! When I finally put down the booze I was terrified to do anything because I was afraid I would stumble into a "high risk" situation and fall off the wagon. At that point, many months had passed since I had done anything fun.

Golf had been a longtime source of fun and relaxation for me. But since I had been unable to complete a round without getting insanely hammered, I had simply given it up. In fact, by the time I got sober I figured I would never play again for the rest of my life. It's just a game, but it had been part of my life for so long it felt like a part of me was missing.

About a month into my sober journey I was talking with a fellow recovering alcoholic. He had been sober for several years and became someone to whom I looked up. As we chatted, the topic of golf came up. We talked about different courses and various tournaments. He suggested we should play some time. I thanked him but politely declined.

The following week he brought it up again. He suggested that spending time on the golf course again might be a healthy way for me to spend my time. I took a chance and accepted.

Those first few rounds were pretty awkward, but eventually I got into the groove. I joined an amateur tour and played in a bunch of tournaments. I was never very good, but I started having fun again. I met lots of new people and started feeling more like the old me.

Addiction took a lot from me…and wanted to take more! But playing that silly game was one way for me to draw a line in the sand and say, "No, addiction, you don't get to make all the rules."

Since then I've developed other hobbies because I want to have fun in sobriety. I gave up alcohol, but I gained SO MUCH more. So, the "what will I do with myself if I quit drinking" is a great question and one I'm happy to address. I hope to adequately answer that question in the next few pages. You shouldn't be expected to give up something that's been a significant part of your life and just be bored and boring.

A client with a long history of alcoholic drinking, "Miles," talks about fun in sobriety all the time. He says, "I have a choice to make every day. I can stay sober or get drunk. If staying sober weren't fun, all I'd have to do is stop in that liquor store right across the street (there's always one right across the street no matter where you are) and grab a bottle. Today I choose not to do that because I'm having too damn much fun living this life!"

I'm not sure I can say it any better than Miles. One promise I've made and will continue to make is that I'll never ask you to give up something without helping you replace it with something better. Nobody would get clean or sober if the alternative was just sitting at home staring at the walls and being miserable.

Let's be honest…you use chemicals such as drugs, alcohol, nicotine, caffeine and sugar for one reason: they change they way we feel in some positive way. Even if you drink or get high to celebrate something positive, you are changing your state from "feeling good" to "feeling great," so it's easy to create a relationship between your drug of choice and "fun."

The problem is that over time, something changes in many of us where we go from *choosing* to use a chemical to *needing* to use a chemical. For example, when someone first smokes a cigarette they may experience a pleasant euphoria from the nicotine. But after they have been smoking for a while, they need a cigarette regularly or they start feeling pretty nasty. This is actually physical withdrawal from the nicotine, and this person has gone from simply wanting to smoke to needing to smoke.

The same pattern is true for those of us who have become dependent on alcohol or drugs. I've heard this story countless times from clients. They tell me at first they drank or used drugs for fun. Their use was social. They gradually used more and more. Then they used by themselves. Eventually, the choice of whether to use or not was gone. The fun had long disappeared and they simply drank or used drugs to keep from becoming sick.

In this chapter we are going to focus on breaking the mental relationship between your drug of choice and "fun." We are going to replace it with a relationship between sobriety and fun. Again, I would never ask you to quit drinking or using drugs and just sit around feeling lonely and miserable.

Strategy 5: FIND A NEW HOBBY

Hobbies may seem like a pointless distraction and a waste of precious time. To the contrary…they are an important part of a well-balanced, healthy life. Finding a hobby you enjoy and that lines up with your aptitudes, values and interests can not only provide distraction but also help you grow emotionally.

At the most basic level, a hobby gives you

something to do during the time you would have been drinking or using drugs. On a more important level, a hobby exposes you to new people, new ways of thinking, new ways of viewing the world, and possibly a new perspective on how you live your life.

Sometimes rediscovering an old hobby is more important than finding a new one. Very often, drinking and drugging takes over your life and squeezes out time for or interest in anything else, including hobbies.

I encourage you to think outside the box and try hobbies that are outside of your usual interests. Remember that growth happens outside of your comfort zone. The only rules are that you can't take up alcohol-related hobbies, so beer home brewing and wine tasting are off the table for you!

Strategy 6: DEVELOP NEW FRIENDSHIPS

You may have had a lot of friends during your party life, or you may have tended toward isolation. Likely the "friends" you knew from the bar aren't going to have much in common with the new, sober version of you. And, like many of us, you may have damaged so many relationships that you don't have friends left. Either way, making new friends is an important aspect of recovery.

This is one of the hardest lessons for many people in early sobriety to internalize. Folks understand it superficially, but when it comes to putting it into practice, they drop the ball. Pay attention to this because it's important. I can't tell you how many people I've seen relapse because they didn't get this important point.

Here it is…**if you are serious about maintaining long-term, high-quality sobriety, you will likely have to change what you do, where you go, and who you spend time with.**

Yes, you may have to cut out friends you've known forever. That sucks? Yeah, I'm with you…it really sucks. But this is one of the points where the men get separated from the boys (and the women from the girls, for that matter). Only someone who is heart-attack serious about getting sober and staying that way will tell their old buddy, "Sorry, I can't hang out with you if you are going to drink/use drugs." It's hard, but it can be done.

How do you do it? Well, to be perfectly honest, many of the people from your "old life" will drift away naturally. Some will have respect for what you are trying to accomplish and give you space. Some will be so self-involved that they don't even notice you are gone. However some, though a small minority, will try to convince you that you are overreacting. They will romanticize the party lifestyle and try to entice you to join them.

This makes sense to me because, in my experience, misery loves company. If your running buddy is stuck, he doesn't want to be stuck alone. My advice to you, which you can ignore at your own peril, is to gently tell him that you will miss him, but that your new lifestyle requires stepping away from anyone who is still using. You can suggest that you and he may possibly renew your friendship down the road. But for now, you are not going to be available for him. Oh, and don't try to save him. As someone who is new to sobriety, all you will do is drown both of you.

Again, I'm going to keep my promise of not telling you to get rid of something without replacing it with something else. Pay attention to other people who might be possible friends. One good starting place is the hobbies from the previous exercise you have been investigating. If someone shares an interest with you, they may make a good friend. Take a risk and strike up a conversation.

Strategy 7: GET OUT OF THE HOUSE

This is more common sense than an actual "exercise," which might make it even more valuable and worthy of your attention.

What if I tell you that you can do anything you like other than scratch your nose? Even if your nose doesn't itch, you will probably want to scratch it. The longer you try to not scratch your nose, the more you will feel pulled to do so. This is a simple analogy to explain an important aspect of addiction: relapse due to boredom.

If you are a person in early recovery, meaning you recently quit drinking and/or drugging, the last thing you need to do is sit home, feel sorry for yourself, and think about *not* drinking/using. That's just torture!

If you sit around trying not to think about your drug of choice, that's just about all you are going to think about. This leads to the sensation of craving, which is that horrible overwhelming compulsion to drink or use. If you've ever tried to quit before, you know exactly what I'm talking about.

The funny thing about cravings is that they have

two possible outcomes. The craving will continue to grow until you finally drink or use the drug (or smoke the cigarette or scratch your nose). When you finally give in to the craving, you feel immediate relief. The problem is that the relief is temporary and when it comes back, it will likely be stronger than before. This leads to that dreaded cycle of use, recovery from use, brief abstinence, anxiety caused by craving, and relapse.

The other possible outcome is actually dealing with the craving in some positive manner, which is what this book is all about. The good news is that every time you experience a craving and don't give in to the temptation, you get stronger. Over time, the frequency and intensity of cravings decreases. An example of a good way to deal with the craving is to get out of the house and keep yourself occupied so you are less likely to experience cravings in the first place.

So, go do something!

I could list hundreds of examples, but I'm confident you can come up with plenty of good ideas on your own. Start by taking the dog for a walk. If nothing else, you'll make Rover's day.

Your Progress So Far

Hopefully you are starting to have some fun at this point. You may be feeling happy and excited. Some people will begin to feel better physically around now, but other folks will still have another few days of discomfort, especially if you have just quit drinking or using drugs in the past week. If you are having fun, just enjoy yourself and be proud of the work you have done so far. If you are still struggling, please hang in there. Getting clean and sober is hard, but I PROMISE the work you put in now will absolutely be worth the effort in the very near future.

Chapter 5 Action Steps:

1. Research three hobbies you might like to try. Actually do one of them within the next week.

2. Strike up a conversation with at least one potential new friend.

3. Get out of the house and stay occupied.

CHAPTER 6: STEPPING OUT OF YOUR COMFORT ZONE

As I got closer to home, I felt increasingly anxious. With every block, my hands sweat more and my stomach twisted into a tighter knot. I had to ask my wife a question and I dreaded doing so.

By that time I had been in an outpatient substance abuse treatment program for about two weeks. Part of the program was "family night." This was an opportunity for clients to invite family members to participate in the treatment process. Of course, family members were not required to attend, but participants were required to extend the invitation.

I knew if I waited too long I would chicken out, so as soon as I walked in the door I blurted it out… "Do you think you would be able to come to a session with me on Tuesday evening?" I held my breath, waiting for a reply.

"Well", she said, "it's kind of short notice and we don't have a babysitter."

"Yeah, I know it's short notice, but it's important."

"Maybe some other time. I don't know who we could get to babysit."

I swallowed hard, looked her in the eye and said, "I know it's inconvenient. I know it's short notice. And I assume you really don't want to go…I don't blame you. If I need to, I'll knock on every door in the neighborhood and call everyone we know to get a babysitter. I really need you for this."

My wife paused, searching my face. "Okay," she said simply, "I'll go."

Asking my wife such a simple question shouldn't be so hard. After all, she was my life partner and soul mate…and had been for a decade!

Why was I so nervous about such a seemingly simple task? Well, I was anxious for good reason.

She had spent the past ten years or so married to an alcoholic. She had heard every unbelievable excuse, every harebrained idea and every pile of nonsense any reasonable person could imagine. She had waited countless times for me to come home after a "quick stop" at the bar. She had grudgingly left me with our daughter, not knowing if I could stay sober enough to be responsible for her safety.

So, given my history, not much I said carried a lot of weight. I had *earned* that level of mistrust. But here's the dangerous part…I internalized it. Let me say that again because it's so important. Not only did I understand *intellectually* that I had messed up, but I experienced *emotionally* that I was no longer worthy.

When I combined these "less-than" feelings with my already precarious emotional state (remember, I had only been sober for about two weeks), I created a recipe for me to really beat myself up. And boy, did I ever beat myself up. I convinced myself everything was my fault, whether I was to blame or not.

This type of emotional booby trap is incredibly

common. The craziest part is that we set the trap for ourselves, then we happily step into it! And we do it again! If you do this enough, it's easy to convince yourself you are useless.

So our goal is for us to stop creating our own emotional booby traps and work toward restoring a sense of usefulness. This chapter contains one exercise that is designed to help you do just that. But first, let's talk about what I learned in prison.

Volunteering for Prison

Standing in the sally port, I could barely see the parking lot. A crackly voice interrogated me: "Please state your business."

"Um, I'm a volunteer. I was told to ask for Warden Sanders."

A few uncomfortable moments passed before a loud click signaled the unlocking of the heavy steel gate. I pushed hard and found myself standing in a narrow grassy area that separated the innermost chain-link fence from the building. I took four or five more steps and found myself facing another heavy steel door. Just as I reached for the handle I was greeted by another loud unlocking click. Passing this threshold I found myself in a small foyer, facing a correctional officer behind a bulletproof window.

The smell immediately took me by surprise. I never realized that the inside of a prison smelled so different; disinfectant mixed with stale air to create a unique odor. It smelled like…captivity. Suddenly I understood that I had stepped into a world of hopelessness.

As I was shown to our meeting room my discomfort evolved first into nervousness, then into full-blown terror. "What the hell have I gotten myself into?"

A split second before my nerve broke and I decided to run for the door, the first pair of inmates ambled through the door. They flashed friendly smiles at me and slipped comfortably into the orange molded plastic chairs. Suddenly, I was calm…remembering why I was there. This evening was about them…not about me.

Over the next two hours or so we shared stories about our battles with addiction. In most cases our situations were different. For the most part those incarcerated addicts were from the lowest rung of the socio-economic ladder. After all, certain groups are way over-represented in prisons across our country. But during the course of our conversation we were able to let our differences melt away. We were able to find common ground and help each other. I'm not sure what good I did during that trip. I'm not sure if I added any value to the lives of any of the inmates. But I know for a fact that I was helped.

Future visits were much easier and eventually I became fairly comfortable in a jail/prison setting (as comfortable as one can get, I guess). Today my work takes me into jails on a regular basis. In fact, a week seldom passes that doesn't find me working with someone in an institution of some sort.

Because of those volunteer experiences, I have become able to walk into a jail and get right to work with a client in need of help. I don't have to wade through the emotional baggage of finding myself in an uncomfortable setting. I don't have to battle my own discomfort and negative biases. I can start being of service immediately. So my experience of volunteering has put me in a position to be better able to help people who suffer from addictive diseases. That, of course, is why I choose to do the type of work I do.

What did I learn in prison? I learned that I wouldn't trade my problems for anyone else's problems because someone always has it worse than me. I learned that I have something to offer, despite feeling "less-than" most of my life. I learned that helping others with absolutely no expectation of payment pays off in huge and unexpected ways.

What can you learn from volunteering? You will never know until you give it a try. I will bet you get as much from volunteering as the people you choose to help.

Strategy 8: RAISE YOUR HAND

This exercise is all about stepping away from you and doing something for someone else. No matter how big of a mess you've made out of your life, you still have something valuable to offer someone else. You can always find another person who can benefit from your efforts.

You are going to volunteer your time to help someone else!

This is one of those deceptively simple projects. It's easy to say, "You should help others." But finding *appropriate* opportunities can be challenging. I say "appropriate opportunities" because volunteering efforts should be in line with your natural skills and values. For example, if you are horrible at math, an opportunity to tutor students in calculus may not be the best route for you. It would likely end in frustration for you and confusion for the student.

On the other hand, you may be really good at a certain sport. Maybe there is an opportunity to coach a team in an underprivileged neighborhood.

Progress So Far

This is where the rubber meets the road, which means this is also where a lot of people begin to experience some fear. For most of us, this type of activity is way outside of our comfort zone. The good news is that the solution for the fear you feel is to get moving and help someone else.

Sergeant Sober wants to talk to you about these most recent exercises. His message is here... http://sergeantsober.com/link3/.

This is one of the most important practices in the whole program. Helping others is a fantastic way to get out of your own head and move forward in your life. It's also scary for some people, which is why I spend so much time talking about it in Sergeant Sober's Online Sobriety Bootcamp.

Chapter 6 Action Steps:
1. Make a list of your abilities.
2. Research volunteer opportunities in your community.
3. Raise your hand and sign up to help an organization that would benefit from your skills.

CHAPTER 7: NARRATIVE THERAPY – THE POWER OF TELLING YOUR STORY

I was already sitting in a chair sipping weak coffee when the other group members filtered in. They chose their "regular" seats in the uneven circle. We exchanged tentative nods and waited for the group therapy session to begin. Those few participants who knew each other chatted quietly. As the newest member I occupied myself with my cup of institutional coffee, squeezing designs into the Styrofoam lip with my fingernail.

An internal groan nearly escaped my lips when the way-too-bubbly group leader glided into the room. What had I gotten myself into? These people didn't get me! Maybe my drinking really wasn't all that bad! Sitting in my own poisonous thoughts, I heard little of what was said.

But that was all about to change.

A professional therapist was conducting the group, but another woman was assisting. She had come into the room after the group started and had not said very much. She watched the members and made occasional notes in a ragged notebook.

Eventually she cleared her throat and introduced herself. She said, "My name is DeeDee and I'm an alcoholic." She went on to talk about how, though she had been sober for over 20 years, she still occasionally struggled with cravings for alcohol. She described the years of lonely, hard drinking. She talked about how alcohol had taken away a career she loved and damaged almost every relationship in her life. She shared the guilt she felt from lying about drinking and the shame she felt from not being able to stop on her own.

Never had I heard someone talk about alcoholic drinking in such a transparent and authentic manner. To me, drinking had become a deep, dark, shameful secret. The way I drank was not fun or entertaining. I drank hard and drank at problems, if that makes any sense. My drinking was desperate and painful and was aimed, even though I didn't know it, at a big hole in my soul.

Looking around the room I expected to see shocked looks on the faces of my fellow group mates. Instead I saw concern and agreement and empathy. I didn't know you could talk about addiction like that. I didn't know you could let it out!

Hearing that story, sitting in that cramped room, changed things for me. For the first time in recent memory I felt something stirring in me. Something warm and pleasant swirled in my belly and spread slowly through my body. It was hope. For the first time (practically ever) I thought, "My God, I might just survive this crazy shit. I might not be one of those guys who just drinks himself to death." This new feeling was difficult to comprehend since I was so used to feeling bad all the time.

Someone had once described me as a "high bottom drunk." To be honest, I found the description pretty insulting. It implied that my problems and struggles were not real or that they were somehow unimportant. Fortunately, the gift of time brings perspective. That perspective allowed me to look back at my drinking life and see how "high bottom" might be appropriate. However, I have come to understand that the concept of a "bottom" is not very helpful.

The truth is that I didn't experience the extreme problems that some alcoholics and addicts live through. I didn't end up in prison or homeless. I didn't lose my job or my family. I was never rushed to the emergency room, clinging to life by the thinnest of threads. But…many of those losses were right around the corner for me. I didn't realize my wife's concerns for me were much deeper than I ever realized. I didn't realize my boss was considering letting me go since my job performance had been suffering for so long. I didn't experience any of those typical bottoms, but I very easily could have. I was just of the lucky ones who pulled the nose of the plane up in time to keep from crashing into the mountain.

My struggles were internal, but I suffered nonetheless. Even as a boy I felt different in some ways. I had friends and did most of the activities of childhood…school, baseball, football, swimming in the summer, riding my bicycle with my brother and our friends, etc. But I still felt like I had a hole in my identity. That hole was filled when I discovered alcohol.

As an adult I continued use alcohol as a tool to keep that hole from emptying again. This practice kept me from developing healthy relationships and from feeling like a success in my professional life. It kept me from ever truly prospering.

I pushed myself hard to have the trappings of a "successful life." And to be perfectly honest, I did a good job of realizing my version of the American Dream. In fact, many people would have been happy to step into my idyllic life. From the outside things looked great. I had a good job and a beautiful home. My wonderful wife and I were blessed with a healthy child. I went to work on time every day, mowed the grass on Saturday and attended church on Sunday. I did everything I was supposed to do.

But I had a dirty little secret…I hated myself for the failure I saw in the mirror. Fear of being found out for the fraud I really was gripped me constantly. I was sure that any day my boss would find out that I really didn't know what I was doing and usher me out of the building. My wife would surely figure out what a loser she had married and disappear with our child. Even the nice people at church would surely shun me if they could see the blackness in my soul.

Despite an outwardly perfect life, I was desperately sad…so I drank. Each evening I poured one glass of bourbon after another into my belly. Every drink filled me with more dread and reinforced what a loser I was. So I drank more. The cycle was self-sustaining and devastating.

Sitting in that room with DeeDee and the other alcoholics and drug addicts changed things for me. When I realized that I might just survive after all, a sense of hope was born in me.

Hope is a powerful weapon. It brings utter destruction to fear, anger and self-loathing. My disease doesn't want me to feel hope because it wants to see me destroyed. But when DeeDee shared her story I felt it in my bones…hope.

And that's why I share my story of addiction and recovery…to help others as I was helped and to help myself grow and prosper in sobriety. Now you, if you have the courage, are going to learn to tell your story for the same reasons.

But first things first – don't run out and tell everyone who will listen about your drug and/or alcohol use. That will just get you dirty looks and your kids un-invited to play groups. That said, the people in your life likely know your history because they lived it with you. So if you run out and say, "Hey everyone, I'm sober now and want to get the rest of the world sober too," you likely won't have much credibility. This is a process and it needs to be handled carefully.

You are going to write your story of addiction and begin to write your story of recovery. Of course, the second part is still being created so you can add to it as you move forward. There is no right or wrong way to write (or tell) your story. I'm going to suggest one method. You can either follow my method or you can simply get out a page and start writing.

Strategy 9: WRITING YOUR STORY OF ADDICTION AND RECOVERY

As always, start by labeling the page with your name and today's date. Remember, I always like to date documents like this. Then just use the following prompts.

When and where were you born?
What was your first experience with drugs or alcohol?
What was your family life like growing up?
Did you progressively use more drugs/alcohol?
What was the first substance you used?
Did you experiment with other drugs/alcohol?
Did you have a particular drug of choice?
What negative impact did your addiction have on your life (DUI, divorce, medical problems,

emotional problems, school or work problems, etc.)?

How did people in your life respond to your drinking/drugging?

Did you ever try to stop using?

How many times did you go to a treatment facility?

Did you ever feel like you were violating your personal values because of your addiction (stealing, lying, cheating, etc.)?

What's the one (or more) thing you did while drunk or high that you most wish you could undo?

Did you ever do anything dangerous while under the influence of a substance?

What was it like for you when things (your addiction, your actions, your life, etc.) were at their worst?

What happened in your life that made you decide to finally get clean and sober?

What steps have you taken (or what activities have you engaged in) that have helped improve your situation? (I.e., what helped?)

What does your concept of the future look like? Is it positive or negative?

What else would you like to add?

If you like, you can download the worksheet I use when I teach this exercise in Sergeant Sober's Online Sobriety Bootcamp.

http://sergeantsober.com/story

If you systematically work through these questions and prompts and offer a robust response to each, you will have a solid beginning to your story. Of course, you will constantly be thinking of items that need to be added. That's fine. This should be a living, breathing document. As you build some solid time in recovery, you will want to add your thoughts on how your life is different. You may want to contrast your addicted life with your sober life. The idea is to share your hope with others so they become empowered to follow in your footsteps.

The most important part of this exercise, as always, is to just get started. Don't overthink it. Don't worry about it. Don't talk about it. Just get out your paper or word processor and go!

The second most important part, and this is VERY important, is to not turn this into a "drunkalog." You don't want to go on for paragraph after paragraph about how this one time you got so high and did such crazy shit, etc. While that sort of detail may make for a great story, it doesn't help people get clean and sober. In fact, talking about past exploits in positive ways, called "romanticizing," can sometimes have the opposite effect. Those sorts of stories can actually trigger people to relapse rather than encourage them to stay sober. Remember, your story is a powerful tool. Use it for good rather than for evil.

An Example or a Warning?

Your life can either be an *example for* or a *warning to* others. You can live a life that causes people to look at you and say, "I wish I was more like him/her." Or you can be the person who causes people to say to their kids, "See…that's why we stay away from drugs and alcohol." You can be an example or a warning…the choice is yours.

You choose the trajectory of your life by paying attention to the small decisions you make every day. Are you going to accept the lunch invitation from someone with whom you used to share "liquid lunches"? Are you going to skip the daily exercises that have contributed to your sobriety up to this point? Are you going to allow others to talk you out of living a sober life? You don't fall off the wagon all at once. It happens gradually.

My Friend "Russell"

My friend "Russell" is an example of what not to do. Unfortunately, he paid a very high price so I could learn a lesson. He had been sober for about nine months when I met him. By all accounts he was doing well in his recovery from a long history of alcoholic drinking. Gradually he began to pull away from the tools he was learning. He spent less time reading helpful literature. He attended fewer self-help groups. He invested less effort connecting to others. He stopped showing up at his volunteer gig at the hospital. Looking back, this is all crystal clear, but these changes were all very subtle at the time. Even those of us who were close to him couldn't put our finger on what was "off" about our friend.

Then one day he announced to me and another friend that he felt like he might have overreacted with this whole "alcoholic" thing. He had decided that he had given the topic much thought and come to the conclusion that he could control his drinking.

That night he bought a bottle of liquor and had a few drinks. The next night he had a few more drinks. Within two weeks he came home with a case of liquor. He ushered his wife out the door and suggested she go visit her sister, saying he needed some time alone to think. His wife grudgingly left, though Russell had left her little option.

After not being able to reach him by phone, Russell's wife returned home. She was not able to get into the house because the door was blocked. She called the police, who broke down the door. They found Russell's body in a bedroom. Apparently, he had had gotten very drunk and fallen, hitting his head on a piece of furniture. Unable to call for help due to his inebriated state and a head injury, Russell had simply bled to death on the floor of his wife's bedroom.

Your Choice

So, the choice is yours. Will your story be uplifting and hope-inspiring? Will your life be held up as an example of what is possible to achieve? Or will your journey be a sad footnote that serves as an example of how not to live a life?

I hope you will choose the former and pass on the latter. Remember, your story is an incredibly powerful tool. I hope you choose to use it to lift someone up.

Progress So Far

This is another point where many people fall back into fear or apprehension. Some worry about putting their "sins" in writing for fear of either exposing their secrets or seeing for themselves, in writing, their many transgressions. I encourage you to be bold! Move forward with courage because you will likely find your mistakes are not as numerous as you originally imagined. Remember, growth only happens when you step out of your comfort zone.

If you can push past the fear and move forward with the "Write Your Story" exercise I predict you will feel a surge of confidence, serenity and gratitude. I hope you see a light at the end of the tunnel and realize you are going to survive. I pray you begin to understand that the good feeling in your belly is hope. Let that hope blossom by sharing it with others!

Chapter 7 Action Steps:
1. Write your story!

CHAPTER 8: NEXT STEPS IN YOUR SOBER JOURNEY

If you have hung in with me to this point, congratulate yourself. I would love to think everyone who needs help with addiction would read this book. I would also love to think everyone who picked up this book read it to the end. I'm not naïve enough to believe either of those thoughts. The truth is, getting clean and sober is hard. Somehow that sentence doesn't do the task justice. More accurately, getting clean and sober is impossible. It's literally an un-doable task. But, people do it anyway.

What's different about those few folks who somehow do the impossible and get clean and sober? As I've said before, the difference between those who die or go permanently insane from their addiction and those who recover and thrive is *ACTION*. People who do something and persist win. So, if you are reading these words, you have done something probably 99 percent of people who struggle with addiction wouldn't bother to do.

Good for you! Be proud of your efforts and optimistic about your outcomes.

If you have worked your way through this book, you have learned some powerful tools that will help keep you sober long enough to allow your brain to begin healing itself. You learned about:

Journaling:

Putting your thoughts down in writing helps you discover who you are and what areas of your life need additional work. When you write down positive thoughts and feelings, such as goals, they become "cemented" in the neural pathways of your brain. Writing is also a form of thinking through problems and can often lead to creative solutions you never would have found otherwise.

Meditation:

You don't have to be a monk to meditate. This

exercise can include repeating a mantra, focusing on a single word or phrase, prayer, or anything else that makes sense to you. Regular meditation is a fantastic tool for quieting a busy mind, building focus and reducing stress.

Positive Qualities:

Becoming aware of the fact that you are not all bad or all good is extraordinarily liberating. The baggage associated with believing you are "a loser" is exhausting to carry around. Likewise, holding yourself up to impossible standards is just as tiring. Finding balance between these extremes leaves energy you can invest in growing as a person.

Gratitude:

You will never move forward in your life until you stop walking around thinking you are entitled to happiness. Filling your mind with gratitude to the point that negative thoughts have no room to exist is the single greatest way to develop a forward-looking, growth-oriented frame of mind.

Hobbies:

Your addictive lifestyle was probably not conducive to maintaining healthy hobbies, so revisiting an abandoned hobby or developing a new hobby is in order. Hobbies will help you explore your passions, introduce you to people with similar values, and let you have fun without drugs or alcohol.

Friendship:

Friendships are a common casualty of an addicted lifestyle. You likely burned some bridges while you were drinking and/or drugging. In other programs I show you how to work on repairing those relationships. Obviously, that can be complicated. For now, seeking out healthy people who support your sober lifestyle is a critical component in staying sober. Remember…you can't take this journey alone.

Getting Out:

Sitting around thinking about *not* doing the *one thing you can't do* is torture…pure torture! So, don't do that. Get out of the house and participate in fun, healthy activities. Preferably, spend time with those healthy new friends you are making. Remember…getting sober is supposed to make your life better, not worse. Sobriety is FUN!

Volunteering:

This is where the rubber meets the road. Volunteering has so many benefits, both to the volunteer and the recipient of the services, that they are difficult to list. Through giving your time to another person, you grow personally and begin to perceive yourself as someone of value. You will start to see yourself as serving others and bringing joy to their lives. Would a "worthless person" do something so wonderful?

Telling Your Story:

The heartbreaking fact is that most people who suffer from drug addiction or alcoholism die from the disease. So we really are talking about a life-or-death topic here. Your story, shared at the right time with the right person in the right way, might just be the last piece of the puzzle that helps someone turn toward sobriety and away from death. Your story is a hugely powerful tool. Never underestimate it.

Bringing It All Together

Now that you've received an overview of the basic sobriety tools, you are probably wondering how these tools and exercises all fit together. There is no 100 percent right way to use the tools. I'll suggest an example of how you could set up your program, but feel free to tweak the details in order to create a program that works for you.

A sample "menu" for a week:

Monday – Journaling
Tuesday – Journaling, Meditation (5 minutes)
Wednesday – Journaling, Meditation (5 minutes), Positive Qualities exercise
Thursday – Journaling, Meditation (5 minutes), Gratitude List
Friday – Journaling, Meditation (10 minutes), brainstorm possible hobbies and volunteer opportunities
Saturday – Journaling, Meditation (10 minutes), commit to inviting a new friend to coffee
Sunday – Begin writing your story, do something fun outside the house

This structure serves a couple of important purposes for you in your new sober life. First, it builds healthy patterns that are *different from* the patterns of your addicted life. When you were in active addiction, you likely experienced significant chaos. In fact, if you are like many of my clients, your life was defined by chaos. In its place, we want to intentionally create a life that is calm and defined by normal, predictable rhythms. Surprises are going to pop up, but a solid foundation makes those surprises manageable.

The second purpose for a schedule like this is based in neuroscience. Your brain will heal itself, given enough time. To be accurate, you must realize your brain will never be able to resuscitate dead cells. However, it will create new neural pathways from healthy cells. These new pathways will duplicate the functionality you lost with the death of the original cells.

I use a traffic analogy to explain this process, called neuroplasticity. Maybe you normally drive from work to home using Elm Street. But today Elm Street is closed due to construction, so you reroute yourself to Maple Street. You still successfully navigate from work to home, just by a different route.

How much time should you spend working on these exercises? Well you probably spent a lot of time "working" on your drug of choice. You likely spent time seeking, acquiring, using, recovering from, and hiding your use. I'm suggesting you invest much less time than that on recovery. Even a modest amount of time spent working on recovery-focused activities will pay off in huge ways.

Notice I only suggest 5 to 10 minutes per day spent on meditation initially. Sitting still for even five minutes is tough for most of us, especially when we are not used to doing so. Like anything else, these new skills require practice to build expertise. For example, start with five minutes of meditation, then slowly increase the time as you become more comfortable. This should be challenging for you, but not frustratingly so.

Remember, after all is said and done, the most powerful tool at your disposal is ACTION! So make it happen!

What's Next?

You've learned these nine useful tools. "So," you may ask, "is this all I need to know to stay sober forever?" As you might guess, this is a simple question with a complex answer. Some people may be able to practice these exercises and enjoy a wonderful, sober life for years to come. However, others may need more.

When I work with clients who are struggling with addiction issues in my private practice, I usually make a few suggestions. I believe the number of viable routes to sobriety is roughly equal to the number of people who want to get sober.

This means no one way is perfect for everyone. It also means many people need to augment their core recovery program with some other tools.

I've developed a matrix of other strategies so I can offer clients a mixture of services that most closely fit their particular needs. The most basic resource I offer is this book. Some folks might like the content of the book but feel they learn better with more detailed instruction delivered via video. For those people I've created the video-based *Sergeant Sober's Online Sobriety Bootcamp*. You can find more information about Sergeant Sober at http://sergeantsober.com.

People who want more interaction can take advantage of *Sergeant Sober's Advanced Tactics*, which is a private mastermind group. Membership in each session is strictly limited to 12 participants. Members join a web-based forum with an anonymous login ID. You then interact with me and with each other on weekly assignments. You also have the option of participating in a weekly group call.

I also offer personal mentoring for those who are most serious about getting sober, staying sober, and being of maximum service to the people around them. This is a monthly engagement that gives participants direct one-on-one access to me. I offer help on very specific, personal challenges.

No matter what level of service you choose, please take a minute to congratulate yourself. By simply reading this book you have done more to improve your life than 99 percent of people in the world. Remember that addiction is a primary, progressive, deadly disease. But you can stop it if you have the courage. Remember…knowledge is power, but action is the powerful agent of change.

Be bold! Take action!

ABOUT THE AUTHOR

<u>Clay Cutts, Founder of EmpowerAble, LLC</u>

Clay Cutts is a social worker, therapist, author and speaker who specializes in the treatment of addictive diseases. Specifically, he helps men and women who find themselves affected in some way by drugs, alcohol or other addictions. Many of his clients struggle with addiction themselves. Others find themselves victimized by the compulsive, addictive behaviors of someone they love. (After all, addiction IS a family disease!)

Either way, Mr. Cutts helps men and women not just conquer addiction, but move way past it and become the best possible version of themselves.

Clay M. Cutts, L.M.S.W.
Founder, Empowerable, LLC
<u>http://claycutts.com</u>
<u>http://sergeantsober.com</u>
<u>https://www.facebook.com/EmpowerAbleLLC</u>
If you found this book helpful please leave a review on Kindle below my book.